ANCIENT CIVILIZATIONS

A DAY IN ANCIENT GREECE

by Janie Havemeyer
illustrated by Cesar Samaniego

Tools for Parents & Teachers

Grasshopper Books enhance imagination and introduce the earliest readers to fun storylines and illustrations. The easy-to-read text supports early reading experiences with repetitive sentence patterns and sight words.

Before Reading

- Discuss the cover illustration. What do readers see?
- Look at the glossary together. Discuss the words.

Read the Book

- Read the book to the child, or have them read independently.
- "Walk" through the book and look at the illustrations. When and where does the story take place? What is happening in the story?

After Reading

- Prompt the child to think more. Ask: What was life like in ancient Greece? What more would you like to learn about ancient Greece?

Grasshopper Books are published by Jump!
5357 Penn Avenue South
Minneapolis, MN 55419
www.jumplibrary.com

Copyright © 2025 Jump! International copyright reserved in all countries. No part of this book may be reproduced in any form without written permission from the publisher.

Library of Congress Cataloging-in-Publication Data

Names: Havemeyer, Janie, author.
Samaniego, César, 1975- illustrator.
Title: A day in Ancient Greece / by Janie Havemeyer; illustrated by Cesar Samaniego.
Description: Minneapolis, MN: Jump!, Inc., [2025]
Series: Ancient civilizations | Includes index.
Audience: Ages 7-10
Identifiers: LCCN 2024024719 (print)
LCCN 2024024720 (ebook)
ISBN 9798892134804 (hardcover)
ISBN 9798892134811 (paperback)
ISBN 9798892134828 (ebook)
Subjects: LCSH: Greece–Civilization–To 146 B.C.–Juvenile literature. | Greece–Social life and customs–Juvenile literature.
Classification: LCC DF78 .H397 2025 (print)
LCC DF78 (ebook)
DDC 938–dc23/eng/20240604
LC record available at https://lccn.loc.gov/2024024719
LC ebook record available at https://lccn.loc.gov/2024024720

Editor: Alyssa Sorenson
Direction and Layout: Anna Peterson
Illustrator: Cesar Samaniego
Content Consultant: Denise Demetriou, PhD; Professor of Ancient Greek History; University of California, San Diego

Printed in the United States of America at Corporate Graphics in North Mankato, Minnesota.

Table of Contents

Greece's Golden Age	4
Ancient Greece Timeline	22
Map of Ancient Greece	23
To Learn More	23
Glossary	24
Index	24

Greece's Golden Age

Parthenon

The year is 432 BCE. It is summer in Athens. This is one of Greece's most important cities. It is named after the **goddess** Athena. Her **temple** is the Parthenon. It looks over the city.

Zeus statue

The **ancient** Greeks have many gods. Zeus is the king of the gods. He has his own temple in Athens. The Greeks believe Zeus controls the weather. They want to make him happy. They bring an ox and sheep to his temple.

Athens is a **democracy**. Male **citizens** meet early in the morning. They **debate** important issues. They vote. Today, they decide whether to kick a leader out of Athens. Each man writes his vote on a broken piece of pottery.

At the market, people talk about issues in Athens. They shop, too. **Merchants** sell fruits and cheeses.

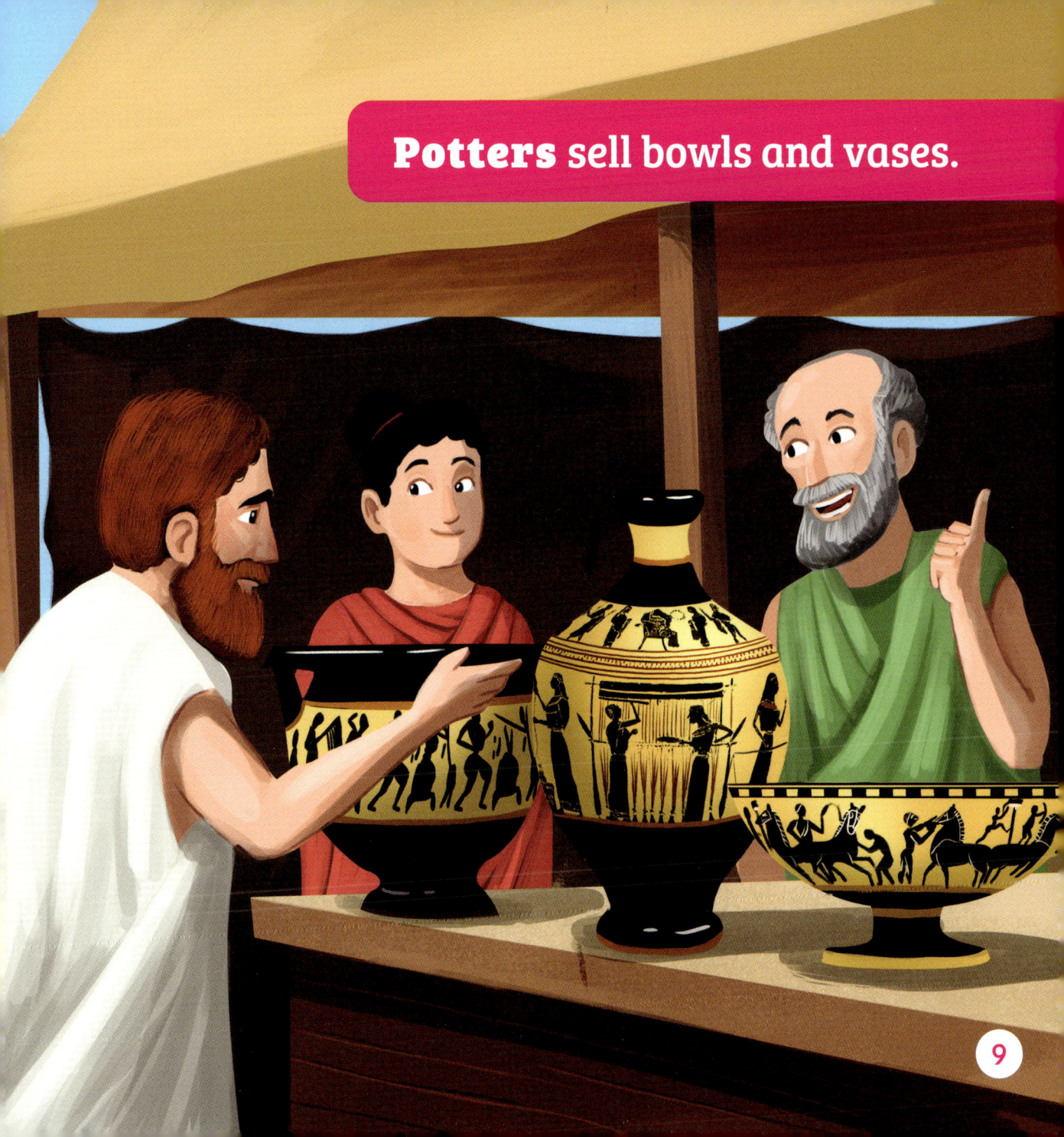

Outside the city, a family works on their farm. They grow wheat and olives to eat and sell. A boy milks a goat. A girl collects chicken eggs.

At school, boys study poetry and practice writing. Music is an important subject, too. They learn to play the lyre.

Girls stay home. They help with chores. One daughter helps her mom weave wool into clothing for the family.

In the afternoon, boys play sports. They swim. They wrestle. They practice shooting arrows with bows. This prepares them to be good soldiers.

Today, there is a chariot race to honor Athena! Riders yell for their horses to go faster. Then the riders jump out. They run next to the chariots. They must jump back in. It is hard to do. People watch and cheer!

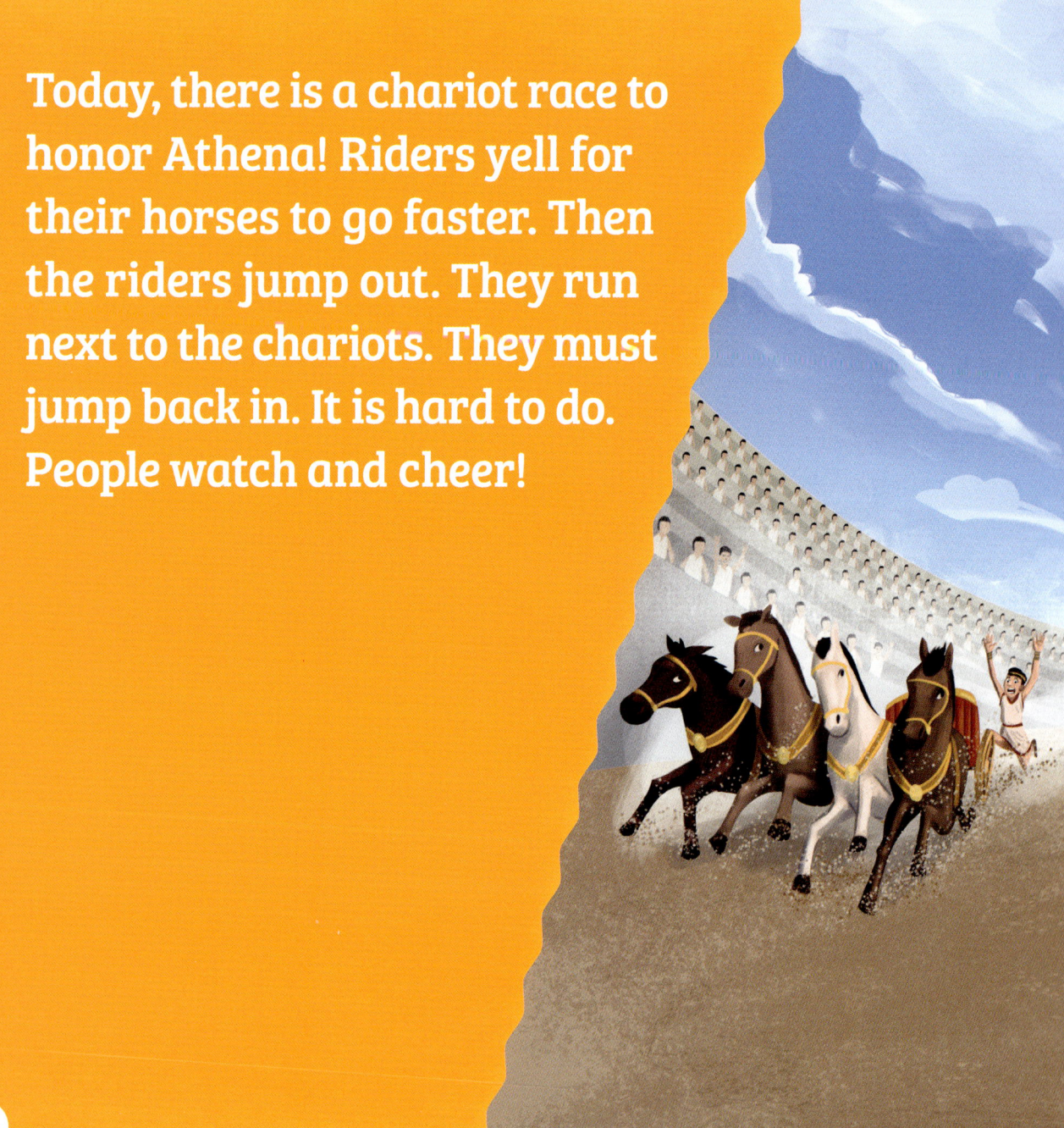

People go to the **theater** to watch a play. Actors wear masks and costumes. People clap when they like something. They hiss when they don't.

At night, a group of men meet for dinner. They lie on couches. They discuss important topics. They eat and drink. A musician performs. Everyone thanks the gods for a good day!

Ancient Greece Timeline

What are some important events in Greece's history? Take a look!

800–500 BCE
Greek cities are built on the coasts of the Mediterranean and Black Seas.

776 BCE
Male athletes compete in a footrace to honor Zeus. The event grows and changes over time. It eventually becomes the Olympic Games.

432 BCE
The Parthenon is completed in Athens. This temple honors the goddess Athena.

508 BCE
Democracy starts in Athens.

380 BCE
The first college in the Western world is built outside Athens.

31 BCE
Greece becomes part of the Roman Empire.

Map of Ancient Greece

Take a look at Greece in 432 BCE.

To Learn More

Finding more information is as easy as 1, 2, 3.
1. Go to www.factsurfer.com
2. Enter "**ancientGreece**" into the search box.
3. Choose your book to see a list of websites.

Glossary

ancient: Very old or from the very distant past.

citizens: Members of a city, town, or country.

debate: To discuss a subject.

democracy: A type of government in which people make decisions by voting.

goddess: A female god, or being that is worshipped and believed to have special powers over nature and life.

merchants: People who make or buy products and sell them to make money.

potters: People who make pottery.

temple: A building in which a god is worshipped.

theater: A place for performances or big events.

Index

Athena 4, 16

Athens 4, 5, 6, 8

chariot race 16

democracy 6

farm 10

lyre 12

market 8

Parthenon 4

soldiers 14

theater 18

weave 13

Zeus 5